Exercise!

FLEXIBILITY

Stretch and Move Further!

Ellen Labrecque

www.raintreepublishers.co.uk
Visit our website to find out more information about Raintree books.

To order:
☎ Phone 0845 6044371
📄 Fax +44 (0) 1865 312263
💻 Email myorders@raintreepublishers.co.uk

Customers from outside the UK please telephone +44 1865 312262

Raintree is an imprint of Capstone Global Library Limited, a company incorporated in England and Wales having its registered office at 7 Pilgrim Street, London, EC4V 6LB – Registered company number: 6695582

Text © Capstone Global Library Limited 2013
First published in hardback in 2013
The moral rights of the proprietor have been asserted.

Edited by Rebecca Rissman, Daniel Nunn, and Sian Smith
Designed by Steve Mead
Picture research by Ruth Blair
Production by Victoria Fitzgerald
Originated by Capstone Global Library Ltd
Printed and bound in China by Leo Paper Products Ltd

ISBN 978 1 406 24202 7 (hardback)
16 15 14 13 12
10 9 8 7 6 5 4 3 2 1

British Library Cataloguing in Publication Data
Labrecque, Ellen.
Flexibility. -- (Exercise!)
1. Joints--Range of motion--Juvenile literature.
2. Exercise--Juvenile literature. I. Title II. Series
612.7'6-dc22

Acknowledgements
We would like to thank the following for permission to reproduce photographs: Alamy p. 29 (© Eileen Langsley Gymnastics); © Capstone Publishers pp. 15, 17, 19, 21 (Karon Dubke); Corbis p. 12 (© Jose Luis Pelaez, Inc./Blend Images); Shutterstock pp. 5 (© Dmitriy Shironosov), 6 (© tankist276), 7 (© Jules Studio), 9 (© fred goldstein), 9 (© YanLev), 10 (© naluwan), 11 (© Buida Nikita Yourievich), 13 (© T-Design), 22 (© Rob Marmion), 23 (© Orange Line Media), 24 (© iofoto), 25 (© Dan Howell), 26 (© Diego Cervo), 27 (© Fotoline), 27 (© Kai Wong), 27 (© Abel Tumik), 27, 27 (© Elena Schweitzer), 28 (© Alexey Fursov).

Cover photograph of a dancer reproduced with permission of Shutterstock (© AYAKOVLEV.COM).

We would like to thank Victoria Gray for her invaluable help in the preparation of this book.

Every effort has been made to contact copyright holders of material reproduced in this book. Any omissions will be rectified in subsequent printings if notice is given to the publisher.

All the Internet addresses (URLs) given in this book were valid at the time of going to press. However, due to the dynamic nature of the Internet, some addresses may have changed, or sites may have changed or ceased to exist since publication. While the author and publisher regret any inconvenience this may cause readers, no responsibility for any such changes can be accepted by either the author or the publisher.

Contents

Some words are shown in bold, **like this**. You can find out what they mean by looking in the glossary.

The wonders of exercise!

Exercise is one of the best things you can do for yourself. It strengthens your whole body. Exercise also makes your **immune system** healthier so that you can fight off colds and the flu.

It can even help you to **concentrate** better. This means that you can do even better at school by making fitness part of your life.

BY THE NUMBERS

Children should avoid being **inactive** for more than two hours in a row in the daytime.

Cycling is a great way to exercise.

5

What is flexibility?

Flexibility is how easily your body and muscles can stretch and bend. The stronger and more flexible you are, the better you'll be at sports such as gymnastics and football.

 You need to be very flexible to carry out some gymnastics moves.

Being flexible also helps athletes avoid injuries caused by stiff or tight muscles. Let's get more flexible!

Injuries caused by tight muscles can be really painful.

Stretching safely

Stretching is one of the best ways to become more flexible. Stretching is something you can do anytime and anywhere. But it is important not to over-stretch or stretch beyond what feels comfortable.

If you feel like yelling "Ouch!" during a stretch, you should stop straight away. You should feel **tension** during stretches, but you should never need to shout out in pain.

Stretching should never hurt.

Dynamic stretching

There are two types of stretching exercises that can help you to become more flexible. The first is when you move your body, or part of your body, while you stretch. This is called dynamic stretching.

 You can move your arms around in circles to stretch your arm and shoulder muscles.

These stretches include sports movements, such as a kicking action. This sort of stretch is done before exercise. It helps to reduce the tightness of your muscles.

 If you lean on something when you kick, make sure it is strong enough to hold you up.

Static stretching

The second type of stretching is when your body doesn't move and you hold the position. This is called static stretching. Static stretching exercises make your muscles longer while your body is at rest. You hold a position (such as bending over and touching your toes) for a count of 15.

Static stretching is usually done after exercise, when your muscles are already warm.

This static stretch helps
you to stretch the muscles
in your arms.

Body circles

Body circles help stretch your **core** (stomach), back, and **torso**. Do them as part of your **warm up**. Spread your feet shoulder-width apart and raise your arms over your head. Lean to one side and bring your arms towards the floor whilst bending at your waist.

Continue with your hands moving across the floor to the other side, then upwards. Switch directions and do it again.

MINI CHALLENGE BOX

Do this stretch while singing your favourite song. This will keep you moving for longer and also challenge you to keep breathing smoothly.

Type of stretch:
Dynamic stretch

15

Leg lifts

Leg lifts help to loosen up your legs. Stand beside a wall and rest your left hand on the wall. Lift up your right leg in front of you, and then move it behind you.

Continue moving your leg forwards and backwards. Then, turn around and swing the other leg.

MINI CHALLENGE BOX

Do 20 swings back and forth with one leg. Turn around and do 20 swings with your other leg.

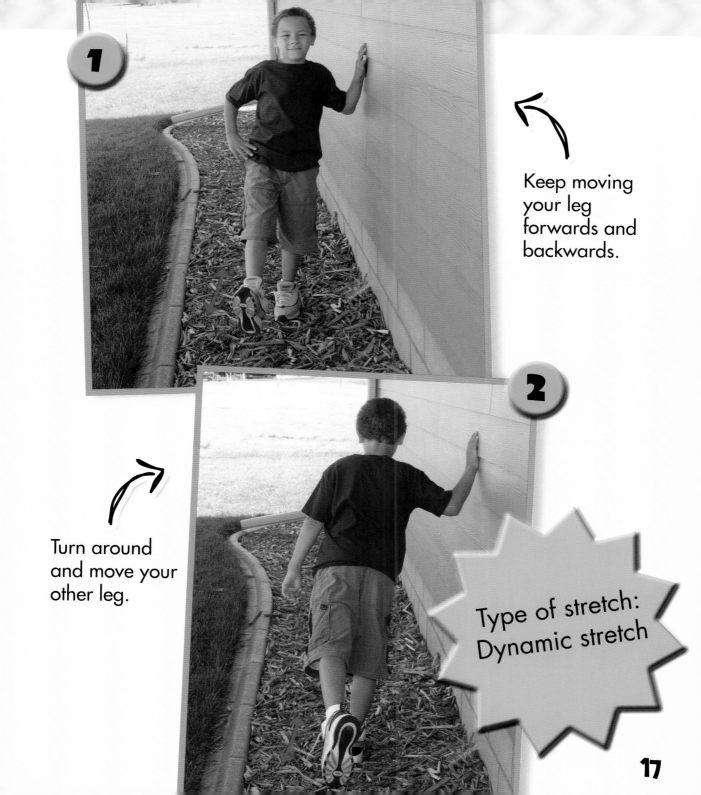

1

Keep moving your leg forwards and backwards.

2

Turn around and move your other leg.

Type of stretch: Dynamic stretch

Butterfly

The butterfly exercise stretches out the inner **thighs** of your legs. Use it as part of your **cool down**. Sit on the floor with the soles of your feet touching each other and your heels pulled in towards your body. Grab your toes and slowly lower your knees towards the floor. Hold for a count of 15.

MINI CHALLENGE BOX

Try to do the stretch three times for 20 seconds each time. Take a break in between each stretch.

Type of stretch: Static stretch

19

Triceps stretch

Triceps are large muscles on the back of your arms. They are used in most sports and it is important to keep them stretched.

Stand with your feet shoulder-width apart. Lift one arm up, bending it at the elbow. Grasp your elbow with your other hand and pull down slightly. Hold for 10 seconds and then switch arms.

MINI CHALLENGE BOX

Try to do the stretch three times for 20 seconds on each arm. Take turns with each arm.

Type of stretch:
Static stretch

21

Yoga time

Yoga is a type of exercise that helps make your whole body more flexible. It is practised by people all over the world to give them better health and more flexibility. It also helps to make them feel happy and peaceful.
Yoga poses are something you can try, too.

People of all ages can learn how to do yoga.

You can look online for ideas, or go to a yoga class in your area.

Many yoga poses help you to build up your strength as well as your flexibility.

BY THE NUMBERS
About 30 million people practise yoga worldwide.

Downward dog

The downward dog yoga pose loosens your back and legs. Start on your hands and knees. Make a tall, upside-down V shape by straightening your legs and putting your feet flat on the floor. Relax your upper chest towards the floor until your arms and body are in a straight line.

Take slow, deep breaths when you are in the downward dog position.

Yoga poses can be safer and more comfortable if you use a mat.

BY THE NUMBERS

There are over 100 different yoga exercises to choose from.

Eating well

Eating certain foods helps you with flexibility. A diet that includes fruit and vegetables can keep your muscles loose. Eating food that has lots of sugar or salt in it can make your joints stiff.

 It is easier to stay flexible when you eat the right foods.

Here is a list of five super foods to help you get more flexible:

1. Blueberries

2. Raw almonds

3. Broccoli

4. Beans

5. Sesame seeds

Big Challenge

The more flexible you are, the better chance you have of becoming a top gymnast. Gymnasts must not only be flexible, they also have to be strong and fast.

To be a good gymnast, you need a combination of strength, balance, and **grace**. If you become flexible enough to bend your body like a rubber band, this will help you with gymnastics, too!

Great gymnasts get to take part in competitions such as the World Gymnastics Championships.

Glossary

concentrate ability to focus on a single task

cool down last part of a workout when the body is allowed to slow down

core centre part of your stomach and back. Your core helps you in almost any movement you make.

grace moving in a beautiful or elegant way

immune system parts of your body that help you fight off illness

inactive not doing anything

tension feeling in the muscles when stretching or straining

thigh part of your leg between your hip and your knee

torso main part of your body. Your head, arms, and legs are joined to your torso.

warm up gentle exercise at the beginning of a workout

Find out more

Books

Exercise (Looking After Me), Claire Llewellyn (QED, 2008)

Gymnastics (Sport and My Body), Catherine Veitch (Raintree, 2010)

Healthy Eating (Health Choices), Cath Senker (Wayland, 2007)

Websites

pbskids.org/itsmylife/body/teamsports/article8.html
This website is a great place to learn the basics of gymnastics.

news.bbc.co.uk/sport1/hi/academy/default.stm
Find out more about famous people in sport.

www.bam.gov
A website devoted to fitness and health for children, including exercise, safety, and eating tips.

Index

WHO LIVED HERE?

My Tudor Home

KAREN BRYANT-MOLE

FRANKLIN WATTS
NEW YORK • LONDON • SYDNEY

© 1995 BryantMole Books
This edition 1998

Published by
Watts Books
96 Leonard Street
London EC2A 4RH

Franklin Watts Australia
14 Mars Road
Lane Cove
NSW 2066

UK ISBN: 0 7496 1962 7
Dewey Decimal Classification Number: 942.05

10 9 8 7 6 5 4 3 2

Design and illustration: Chrissie Sloan
Photographer: Zul Mukhida

Consultant: David Martin, Field Archaeology Unit,
University College London

Acknowledgements
The author and publisher would like to thank Mr and Mrs C. D. Harbour,
the Corliss family and the Dean family for their help with this book.
Photographs: Bridgeman Art Library (Belvoir Castle) 4, Chapel Studios 19 (top),
25 (top), Edinburgh University 17 (bottom), David Martin 13 (bottom), 15 (top),
23 (top), 25 (bottom), 29 (top), Mary Evans Picture Library 5 (both), Mary Rose
Trust 11 (bottom), 13 (top), 15 (bottom), 19 (bottom), 21 (bottom),
Paul Russell 11 (top), 21 (top), 27 (top).
The following pictures are reproduced by kind permission of the Weald and
Downland Open Air Museum, Singleton, 11 (top), 13 (bottom), 15 (top),
21 (both), 23 (top), 25 (bottom), 27 (both), 29 (top).

Printed in Malaysia

Contents

Some of the more difficult words are explained in the Glossary on page 31.

The Tudor Age

The word 'Tudor' means people who lived or things that were made during the time that members of the Tudor family were the kings and queens of England.

The first of the Tudor kings was Henry VII. He became king in 1485. He was followed by his son, Henry VIII. This is a picture of Henry VIII. Henry VIII married six times. He had three children who all became kings or queens. Elizabeth I was the last of the Tudor family to reign. She died in 1603. So, anything that lived or was made between 1485 and 1603 could be called Tudor.

The Reigns of the Tudor Kings and Queens

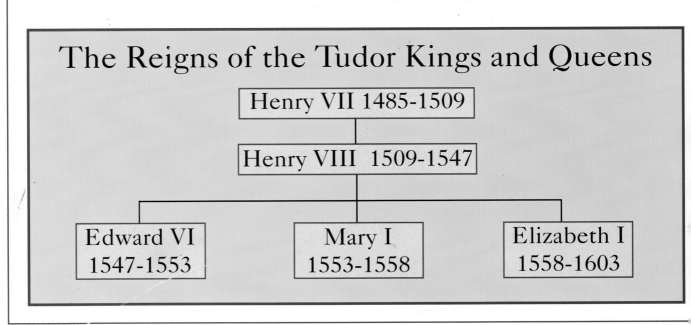

Henry VII 1485-1509

Henry VIII 1509-1547

| Edward VI 1547-1553 | Mary I 1553-1558 | Elizabeth I 1558-1603 |

Tudor people

Many people were yeomen who had land that they farmed. Some people were craftsmen who made things for other people to use or wear. Some were tradesmen, like the bakers in this picture. Other people were merchants, who bought things, like cloth or wine, from one person and sold them on to other people. Most craftsmen, tradesmen and merchants also had a little land that they would have farmed to provide food for their families.

Everyday life

Life in Tudor times was very different to life today. There was no electricity, gas or oil. There were no cars or trains or buses.

Can you imagine what your life would be like without any of these things? People travelled on foot, on horseback or by horse and cart.

Everything, from cooking pots to clothes, had to be made by hand.

The Tudor name for a house was a messuage. Some Tudor houses were built from stone or hand-made bricks but very many were

built around wooden frames. This book will tell you a bit more about one particular timber-framed house.

Moorfoots

The house in the photograph is called Moorfoots. This is what Moorfoots looks like today.

How can we tell that Moorfoots is a Tudor house?

Its black and white striped front wall is a good clue. The black stripes are part of the house's original timber, or wood, frame. The gaps in between the timber frame are filled with something called daub. Daub was a mixture of clay, chopped straw, a white powder called lime and cow dung.

Another clue is the way in which the roof sticks out over the front wall. There were no gutters in Tudor times. If the edge of the roof had been joined on to the top of the front wall, any rainwater would have run straight off the roof and all down the front of the house. The overhanging lip meant that rainwater rolled off the roof and down onto the street.

Moorfoots was built in 1517, when Henry VIII was king.

This is what Moorfoots probably looked like when it was first built. The top part of the house still looks very similar. But can you see the difference in the bottom part? When Moorfoots was first built, the ground floor wall was set further back. The first floor stuck out over the ground floor, in the same way that the roof still sticks out over the first floor. This is called jettying. The front door was in a different place too. When the new front wall was built, the door was moved further down the house.

Although this house was built nearly 500 years ago, we know quite a lot about the way that people lived their lives at that time. This information comes from documents, pictures, buildings and objects that have survived from the Tudor Age.

My Home

Here are the Dean family. They are the people who now live in this house. Sam is the oldest child. Next to him you can see his sister, Abigail. Behind him are his mum and dad. Sam's mum is carrying his brother, Archie.
You will discover more about Sam, his family and their Tudor home as you read through this book.

This is the family that first lived in Moorfoots. They were called the Jordens. The Jordens had four children. There were two boys, called John and Edward, and two girls, called Anne and Mary. A servant lived in the house with them. His name was James. Mr Jorden was a cordwainer. This was the Tudor name for a shoemaker. Mr Jorden used part of Moorfoots as a shop.

These drawings show you the plan of the upstairs and downstairs of Moorfoots when the Jordens lived there. You can look at the plans as you read the book. They will help you to work out where you are in the house.

The
Downstairs
Plan

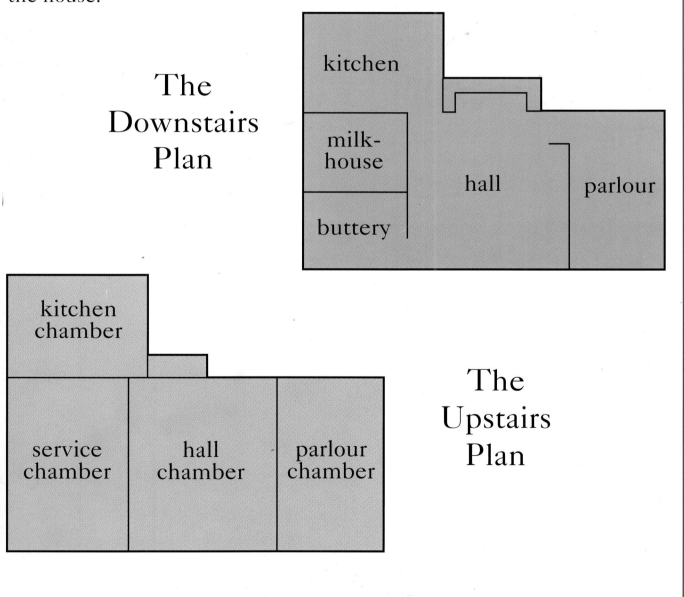

The
Upstairs
Plan

The Hall

This is what the room looks like now. Sam's family call it their lounge. Can you see the television set? The remote control is on the table.

The floor was just an earth floor. Instead of having carpets or rugs, as we do today, the Jordens spread long grasses, called rushes, over the floor. When the rushes got too old or dirty they were swept out and new rushes were laid down.

This room used to be called the hall. It was the main living room of the house. Moorfoots had a huge fireplace. A wood fire was laid in the fireplace. It provided almost the only heat in the house. Some of the rooms got very cold at night and in winter. You can still see the fireplace in the Deans' lounge. The Deans sometimes have a fire too, but their woodburning stove is mostly for decoration. The house is now heated by central heating.

Open fires

This photograph shows you what an early Tudor hall might have looked like. Many homes still had an open fire in the middle of the hall. The table was called a trestle table. It was a large piece of wood laid across two sets of wooden legs. Behind the table is a woven hanging cloth. The Tudors used hanging cloths to decorate plain walls.

Pewter

Tudor families usually displayed the best things that they owned. The objects were laid out on shelves or chests. Pewter plates like these would certainly have been put on show.

The Parlour

Sam's dad is an artist. He uses this room as his studio. You can see some of his pictures at the bottom of the photograph.

Mr Jorden used this room for his job too. It was his shop and workroom. Instead of the customers coming into the shop to be served, they were served through a hatch. A folding counter opened out into the street. Can you see the tools on the table? Shoemakers still use tools like these today.

Of course, only a few Tudor families used their parlour as a shop. In most Tudor homes the parlour was a groundfloor bedroom which also acted as a smaller living room.

Can you see all the beams in the ceiling? The long beam is called a dragon beam. It gives the other beams a special fan shape. This arrangement of beams helped to support the overhanging upper walls.

Shoes

The shoe in this photograph was worn by a sailor on a Tudor ship called the Mary Rose. It is made from leather. The slits in the sides made the shoe bend easily.

Furniture

Here is a copy of a Tudor table and stool. This style of stool is called a boarded stool. The legs on a boarded stool look like short planks of wood.

Most early Tudor furniture was simple and plain but rich people might have had some carved furniture. All Tudor furniture was hand-crafted.

The Buttery

The Jordens called this room the buttery. It was used to store pots, dried food and barrels of ale. The word 'buttery' doesn't come from 'butter' but from 'butt', which was the name given to the barrels where the ale was stored. Ale was a drink that was a bit like beer except that it was made using malt, rather than hops. Most households brewed their own ale. The only furniture in the buttery was a fixed bench and some shelving. There were no fridges or freezers in Tudor times. Instead, latticed wood was put across the buttery window. This kept the room safe from animals but let air blow through and cool the food and ale.

This is Sam and Abigail's playroom. Sam enjoys rollerbooting. They both love reading books.

Herbs

This room has been made to look like a Tudor buttery. There is a barrel of ale on the floor and there are herbs hanging up to dry. The Tudors used a lot of herbs in their cooking. The wooden buckets would have been used to carry water from the well in the garden.

Flagons

These Tudor pottery flagons could have been stored in a buttery. They may have been used for wine. As well as pottery, the Tudors also used pewter, leather, wood and horn to make drinking and storage vessels.

The Milkhouse

Sam's family use this as a music room. Sam's dad plays the trumpet. Sam plays the violin.

Salted meats would have been kept in the milkhouse, too. Salting meat was a good way to stop meat from going bad quickly.

Behind the wall on the right of the picture there was a staircase that led to another, larger, storeroom upstairs. That wall and staircase are no longer there. But, if you look at the ceiling in the Deans' music room, you can still see where the staircase went.

This room was called the milkhouse. It was used for storing milk, making cheese, and churning butter. Mrs Jorden did all the dairy work. Most Tudor women had to work very hard. Each day Mrs Jorden had to milk the cow, feed the animals, collect the eggs, make the cheese and butter, look after the children, brew the ale and do the washing and cooking.

Butter

This drawing shows a woman with a butter churn. Cream that had been skimmed from the top of the milk was put into the wooden churn. Then the cream was moved around very quickly inside the butter churn. The fat in the cream turned into big blobs of butter which were shaped into pats. The thin milk that was left was called buttermilk.

Lute

Sam's dad plays the trumpet. Mr Jorden might have played a musical instrument too. This is a photograph of a lute. It was one of the most popular Tudor instruments. The lute was held across the body, like a guitar, and plucked with the fingers.

The Kitchen

This room is now the dining room. Can you spot Archie's highchair? In the background you can see the Deans' kitchen. Their kitchen isn't part of the original house. It is an extension.

The Tudors built extensions too! When the house was first built its kitchen was in a separate building, close to the house. The Jordens, like many of their friends, decided to build a new kitchen on to their house.

All the cooking was done over an open fire. If the Jordens needed to have something baked, they took it to the baker and he put it into his oven for them.

The Jordens used cooking pots, cauldrons and skillets. A skillet was a saucepan on three legs. It stood right over the fire. Cooking pots often had short legs too. Cauldrons usually had a handle. The handle could be hooked on an iron stand, called a pot crane. This let the cauldron hang over the fire. Some homes had pot hooks. The pot hook hung from an iron bar inside the chimney breast.

Cutlery

The Deans' cutlery is made from stainless steel. This copy of a Tudor spoon is made from pewter. Tudor people did not have forks and often carried their own, personal, knife around with them. Tudor people used their fingers to eat much of their food.

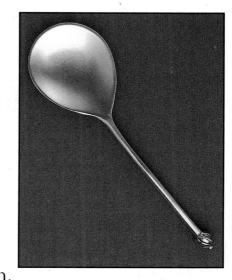

Cooking pots

This is a Tudor cooking pot. It is made from copper. It was possible to cook a whole meal in one cooking pot. Meat, vegetables, dumplings and puddings could all have been hung in nets or skins, around the inside of the cooking pot.

The Parlour Chamber

This is Archie's bedroom. It is half of what was the parlour chamber. The other half is now a bathroom.

Can you see the spinning wheel? Mrs Jorden would have used this to spin wool for cloth and blankets.

This room had a painted cloth on the wall. The hall was decorated with a woven wall hanging. Wall hangings and painted cloths were a way of showing how well off you were.

The parlour chamber was the best bedroom in the house. Its beams were carved and the daub on the walls had a scratched pattern in it, called combing. If you look very closely at Archie's bedroom wall, you may be able to see the combed daub.

Mr and Mrs Jorden slept in this room. They had a big wooden bed with curtains around it. These helped to keep Mr and Mrs Jorden warm at night.

Truckle bed

This photograph shows you what a Tudor bedroom might have looked like. The smaller bed, with wheels, is called a truckle bed. Truckle beds were stored under the main bed. They might have been used by some of the children in the family or brought out when visitors came.

Chest

Tudor homes usually had lots of chests. They were used for storing clothes, linen and household objects. The chest in this picture is made from oak.
It is boarded, which means that it is made from boards that have been pegged together.

The Hall Chamber

The Jorden children slept in this room. They had to walk through their parents' room to get to and from their bedroom. The two girls shared one bed and the two boys shared the other bed. The beds had linen sheets and woollen blankets. The mattress was filled with flock. Flock comes from sheep's wool.

The children were lucky to have a fireplace in their bedroom. This was very unusual for a Tudor home.

There were two small mats on the floor, made from plaited rush stems. The only other pieces of furniture in the room were storage chests.

The upstairs rooms, which were called chambers, took their names from the rooms they were above. This room was above the hall, so it was called the hall chamber.

This bedroom is used by Sam's mum and dad. They have a duvet on their bed and a fitted carpet on the floor.

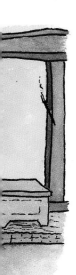

Crib

If there was a baby in the family, he or she might have slept in a wooden cradle like the one next to the bed in this picture. The main part of the cradle hung between the two ends and the baby could be rocked to sleep.

Lighting

The Tudors used candles or rush lights to light their homes. They were held in stands like this. Rush lights were made by soaking dried rush stalks in hot, melted grease and letting the grease dry. Candles had a wick made from rush or twisted cloth. They were dipped into hot grease or wax, over and over again.

The Service Chamber

The room that was the service chamber has been divided up into an office for Sam's mum and a second bathroom.

In Tudor homes the two types of room were usually kept separate. Even though the service chamber was next to the hall chamber, the Jordens could not walk through from one room to the other. Instead they had to go down the stairs, through the hall, into the parlour, up the stairs into the parlour chamber and through to the hall chamber.

The Jordens' service chamber did not have a ceiling. It was open to the roof. They used the room as a storage area for things like corn and fruit. Mr Jorden kept the leather for his shoes here too.

The buttery and the milkhouse were known as service rooms. This room was above the service rooms, so it was called the service chamber. These rooms were work rooms rather than living rooms.

Chamber pots

Part of the service chamber is now a second bathroom and loo. The Jordens didn't even have one loo in their house. At night Tudor people would have used a chamber pot. This is a photograph of a Tudor chamber pot. It was a bit like a potty, but it was used by both adults and children.

Garderobe

Tudor loos were usually just a pit in the garden. A few houses had a garderobe, like the one in this photograph. A garderobe was a small, cupboard-sized area, that was built out from an upstairs bedroom. It had a loo seat but everything that went through the seat just fell down, through the open air, into a pit!

The Kitchen Chamber

James, the servant, slept in here. His mattress was stuffed with straw and his sheets were made from a cream-coloured linen, called unbleached linen. James had lots of different jobs to do around the house and garden. He would have done all the heavy work, such as chopping wood for the fires.

James was the eldest son of Mrs Jorden's brother. In Tudor times, servants were often the sons of relatives and friends. Living with and working for another family was considered to be part of growing up.

Many servants were apprentices too. In return for his work as a servant, Mr Jorden taught James how to make shoes.

This is Sam and Abigail's bedroom. Can you see the radio cassette player on the chest of drawers? Both the children like listening to story tapes.

Stools

Tudor people usually sat on stools. This type of stool is called a turned stool. It gets its name from its wooden legs, which have been 'turned', or shaped, by the craftsman who made it. Three-legged stools were very popular because they didn't wobble on the uneven floors.

Windows

Most Tudor homes had windows with no glass in them. The windows had wooden frames, with thin, wooden bars to stop animals or people climbing in. Wooden shutters were used to close up the windows at night.

The Garden

Moorfoots now has quite a small garden. There are paved pathways and pretty flowerbeds. There is a bird table in the garden too.

The Tudors grew lots of different herbs. Some, like sage and tarragon, were used to flavour food. Some, such as rue and liverwort, were used as medicines. Other herbs, like lavender and sweet briar, were used inside the house, to make the rooms smell nice.

When Moorfoots was first built it had a large yard and garden. It was divided into smaller areas by fences and hedges. These areas were called closes. The Jordens kept pigs, hens, a cow and a horse. You can just see the top of the Jordens' cart.

There were no lawns in the Jordens' garden, just stone pathways and beds for the plants. The Jordens grew vegetables like turnips, carrots and cabbages, and salad ingredients, such as cress and radishes.

Bee hives

Many Tudor homes had bee hives. These hives have been made in the style of Tudor hives. Sugar was extremely expensive so, instead, families used the honey from the hives to sweeten their food.

Wells

This picture shows someone collecting water from a well. For most households, using a well was the only way to get water.

The woman at this well has to haul on the rope to pull up the bucket. Wooden buckets full of water are very heavy. Aren't we lucky that nowadays we can just turn on the tap?

Things to Do

Painted cloth ▲

You can make a painted cloth using a piece of old sheet or pillowcase. (Make sure you ask first.) Cut the cloth to the size you want. Place it on some newspaper. You can either paint your pattern freehand, using a paintbrush, or print your pattern. You can make Plasticine prints by moulding Plasticine into a shape and dipping the end into some paint. You can make block prints by sticking shapes cut from cardboard onto small wood blocks, or you could make potato prints by cutting away pieces of potato to leave a raised shape.

Weaving

The hanging cloth in the picture below is woven. See how weaving works by making your own woven hanging using coloured paper. You will need two A3-sized pieces of coloured paper. On one piece, draw six or seven evenly-spaced lines, lengthways, from about 3cm from the top to about 3cm from the bottom. Carefully, cut along the lines. Cut the other piece of paper into strips, widthways. Weave the strips in and out of the slits in the first piece of paper. Take it in turns to weave one strip over then under and so on, and the next under then over. Glue down the ends. ▼

Butter ▲

Try making your own butter by putting some cream, or creamy milk, into a screw-topped jar. Put the lid on and shake the jar as hard as you can. After a while the cream will start to separate. Keep shaking and eventually you will end up with some blobs of butter. Strain off the buttermilk and make a sandwich, using your own home-made butter!

Glossary

apprentice	someone learning a craft or trade
cauldron	a round cooking pot
close	an enclosed piece of land
combing	a decoration made by scratching a design into daub
cordwainer	a shoemaker
craftsman	someone who makes things
cutlery	knives, forks and spoons
dairy	to do with milk
daub	a clay-based mixture used in house building
document	written information
flagon	a type of container used to hold liquids
flock	poor quality wool
garderobe	a type of loo
latticed	with a criss-cross pattern
linen	a material that is a bit like cotton but is made from flax
merchant	someone who buys and sells goods
messuage	a house, often with outbuildings and some land
pewter	a metal made from tin and lead
skillet	a cooking pot with legs and a long handle
tradesman	a shopkeeper
Tudor	anyone who lived or anything that was made between 1485 and 1603
unbleached	has not been whitened
vessel	a name given to containers that hold liquids
woven	made by weaving threads over and under other threads
yeoman	someone who works on his own land

Index